Tiny Teeny Halloweeny Treasury

Tiny Teeny Halloweeny Treasury

Mary Engelbreit

with patrick regan

**Andrews McMeel
Publishing**

Kansas City

www.andrewsmcmeel.com

www.maryengelbreit.com

 is a registered trademark of Mary Engelbreit Enterprises, Inc.

Engelbreit, Mary.
    Tiny teeny halloweeny treasury / Mary Engelbreit with Patrick Regan.
      p. cm.
    ISBN 0-7407-1873-8
    1. Halloween. I. Regan, Patrick, 1966- II. Title.
GT4965 .E53 2001
394.2646--dc21   2001022276

01 02 03 04 05 MON 10 9 8 7 6 5 4 3 2 1

Illustrations by Mary Engelbreit
Edited by Patrick Regan
Design by Stephanie R. Farley

Halloween's the one time
  Simply, purely fun time;
Full of superstitions
  Born of old traditions
Gnome and elf and fairy,
  Witch and ghost make merry
On this last of dear October's days.

—Halloween Happenings, 1921

table of contents

October

introduction

I love Halloween! I loved it as a kid, and I love it even more today. Halloween is the perfect topper to autumn. It's an outing to a pick-your-own pumpkin patch . . . it's spending very little money but way too much time on homemade costumes . . . it's watching normal suburban lawns transformed into creepy pretend cemeteries. To me, Halloween is a triumph of silliness (with a little scariness thrown in just for fun). And let's not forget the decorations, the parties, and the eatable treats—crisp red apples, pumpkin pie, spiced cider . . . and if there's a more perfect food than candy corn, I haven't found it yet!

The images of Halloween have always provided a rich source of artistic inspiration. I can't begin to guess how many times as a child I drew that classic Halloween scene . . . a witch, riding a broomstick, silhouetted in front of a full harvest moon. I probably drew it for the first time at age 8, and I'm still perfecting it to this day!

Dressing up at Halloween is something I've never been able to resist. When I was only two-and-a-half years old, my mother dressed me up as a gypsy for Halloween. She said that I stared into the mirror and said, "It doesn't look like Mary anymore." I still love that about Halloween—after all, who doesn't want to be somebody else once in a while—if only for one day. That's the best thing about this holiday—it's grown up right along with us. We don't have to enjoy it vicariously through our kids—we get to act just like them!

I've wanted to do a book about Halloween for a long time. And, like a trick-or-treat bag at the end of a long night's trek, I wanted it to be overflowing with delicious, fun, and surprising goodies such as the super (but not super scary) glow-in-the-dark endsheets. Open the cover of the book to expose the black paper to light, then go to a dark place in your house and watch as ghosts begin to glow! This book collects lots of my Halloween art along with many favorite Halloweeny writings, both old and new. There are recipes perfect for the season, stories about the origins of favorite Halloween customs and traditions, Halloween songs you might remember from grammar school, and even silly Halloween jokes and a spooky story or two.

I hope you have as much fun spending time with this book as I had putting it together. Happy Halloween!

Yours Boo-ly,

Scary Mary
Engelfright

To Pumpkins at Pumpkin Time

Grace Cornell Tall

Back into your garden-beds!
Here come the holidays!
And woe to the golden pumpkin-heads
Attracting too much praise.

Hide behind the hoe, the plow,
Cling fast to the vine!
Those who come to praise you now
Will soon sit down to dine.

Keep your lovely heads, my dears,
If you know what I mean . . .
Unless you want to be in pie,
Stay hidden or stay green!!

Pumpkin Patch

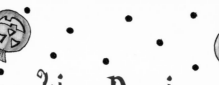

Pumpkin Recipes

Pumpkin Muffins

Wash leftover pumpkin carvings with water.
Bake carvings at 350° for 30 minutes or until soft.
Cool the pumpkin pieces, peel and mash in a bowl.
Mix together in a separate bowl ³/₄ cup flour, ¹/₄ cup honey,
¹/₄ teaspoon salt, 1 tablespoon baking powder, ¹/₄ teaspoon
cinnamon and ¹/₄ teaspoon nutmeg.
Add 1 egg, 2 tablespoons of milk, ¹/₄ cup of pumpkin and
¹/₈ cup of butter. Mix well.
Spoon batter mix into muffin tins and sprinkle with sugar.
Bake at 400° for 20 minutes. Let cool before serving.

Pumpkin Cookies

Ingredients:
- ½ lb. butter
- 2 cups brown sugar
- ½ cup white sugar
- 4 eggs
- 2 cups mashed cooked pumpkin
- 1 tsp. vanilla
- 2 cups chocolate chips

Sift together:
- 4 cups flour
- 4 tsp. cinnamon
- 1 tsp. salt
- 1 tsp. cloves
- 1 tsp. nutmeg
- 1 tsp. ginger
- 2 tsp. baking soda

Cream together: butter, sugar, eggs, and pumpkin.
Add dry ingredients.
Blend in vanilla and chocolate chips.
Drop by spoonful onto greased cookie sheet.
Bake at 400° for 10-12 minutes.

Pumpkin Facts

■ A pumpkin is really a squash. It is a member of the Cucurbit family which includes squash and cucumbers.

■ Pumpkins are grown all over the world except in Antarctica. They are even grown in Alaska.

■ Pumpkins are believed to have originated in North America. Seeds from related plants found in Mexico date back over 7000 years to 5500 B.C.

■ Native American Indians used pumpkin as a staple in their diets centuries before the Pilgrims landed. Pumpkin soon became a staple in their diets as well. Just like today, early settlers used pumpkins in a wide variety of recipes from desserts to stews and soups.

■ The word "pumpkin" dates back to the 17th Century. It comes from the Old French, "pompion," in its turn derived from the Greek word for melon, "pepon," meaning "cooked by the sun," or ripe.

Scarecrow

Five Little Pumpkins

Five little pumpkins sitting on the gate.
The first one said, "Oh my it's getting late!"

The second one said, "There are witches in the air!"
The third one said, "But we don't care!"

The fourth one said, "I'm ready for some fun!"
The fifth one said, "Let's run, and run, and run!"

Then . . . "Oooh" went the wind
And OUT went the light,
And the five little pumpkins rolled out of sight!

Pumpkin Poem

One day I found two pumpkin seeds.
I planted one and pulled the weeds.
It sprouted roots and a big, long vine.
A pumpkin grew; I called it mine.
The pumpkin was quite round and fat.
(I really am quite proud of that.)
But there is something I'll admit
That has me worried just a bit.
I ate the other seed, you see.
Now will it grow inside of me?

(I'm so relieved since I have found
That pumpkins only
grow in the ground!)

Halloween Facts
The Strange (but not too scary) True History of Halloween

■ The word "Halloween" originated in the Catholic Church. It is a form of "All Hallows Eve," which is the night before All Saints Day. "All Hallows Eve" eventually became known as "Halloween."

■ The celebration that occurs on October 31 actually predates the church by more than a thousand years by incorporating traditions both religious and pagan.

■ The origin of Halloween dates back more than 2000 years to Celtic Ireland. The holiday was called Samhain (pronounced "sow-en"), and was a celebration of the dead. A Celtic festival was held on November 1, honoring the Samhain, the Lord of Death.

■ The Druids, (Celtic religious leaders), believed that the Samhain permitted ghosts, witches, goblins and other spirits to spend the Celtic New Year's Eve (October 31) wandering freely.

■ The Druids lit bonfires, gave gifts of special food, and disguised themselves in masks and costumes, believing that the spirits, who were free for only one night, would not recognize them and thus could do them no harm.

■ One story says that on the evening of October 31, the disembodied spirits of all who died would come back in search of living bodies to possess for the next year. The villagers would extinguish the fires in their homes, to make them cold and undesirable to the spirits.

■ The custom of trick-or-treating is thought to have originated with a European custom called "souling." On November 2, All Souls Day, early Christians would walk from village to village begging for "soul cakes," made out of square pieces of bread with currants. The more cakes the beggars would receive, the more prayers they would say on behalf of the donor's dead relatives.

Orange and Black Facts

The traditional colors of Halloween
reflect the twin roots of this ancient holiday.

■ **Orange**, with its suggestion of ripened fruits,
vegetables and grains, reminds us that Halloween
was originally a harvest festival.

■ **Black** evokes images of black magic, witches,
cats and the mystery of Halloween—a direct link to
the time when Halloween was celebrated as a
festival for the dead and night for the gathering of
evil spirits, witches and ghosts.

Bedtime
Anti-Monster Checklist

1. Look under bed!
2. Check in closet. (Close door tightly!)
3. Check night-light operation.
4. Re-check under bed.
5. Put covers over head.
6. Think happy thoughts!

The Legend of the Jack-O'-Lantern

The legend of the jack-o'-lantern goes back hundreds of years in Irish history, and was brought to America by the first Irish immigrants.

Stingy Jack was a miserable old drunk who liked to play tricks on everyone: family, friends, his mother and even the Devil himself. One day, he tricked the Devil into climbing up an apple tree. As soon as he did, Stingy Jack placed crosses around the trunk of the tree. Unable to get down the tree, Stingy Jack made the Devil promise him not to take his soul when he died.

When Jack finally died, he went to the pearly gates of heaven and was told he was too mean and too cruel and had led a miserable and worthless life on earth. He was not allowed to

enter heaven. He then went down to hell and met the Devil. The Devil kept his promise and would not allow him to enter hell. Now Jack was scared and had nowhere to go but to wander about forever in the darkness between heaven and hell. He asked the Devil how he could leave as there was no light. The Devil tossed him an ember from the flames of hell to help him light his way. Jack placed the ember in a hollowed out turnip, one of his favorite foods which he always carried around with him whenever he could steal one. From that day on, Stingy Jack roamed the earth without a resting place.

On All Hallow's Eve, the Irish hollowed out turnips, rutabagas, gourds, potatoes and beets and placed a light in them to ward off evil spirits and keep Stingy Jack away. These were the original jack-o'-lanterns. In the 1800's, a couple of waves of Irish immigrants came to America. The Irish immigrants quickly discovered that pumpkins were bigger and easier to carve out, so they began using pumpkins for jack-o'-lanterns.

The Pumpkin's Wish

Elsie E. Thornburg

"I want to be a punkin face,"
    A pumpkin one day said,
"I'd hate to be a punkin pie—
    The heat would hurt my head.

"I'd rather sit upon a post
    And be a shining light;
I'd want a candle in my head
    Ere I went out at night.

"I'd keep a grin upon my face
    No matter what I did;
My mouth would stretch from ear to ear—
    'Twould scare most any kid.

"My eyes would shine like two bright stars,
    They'd pierce a person through;
My teeth would be all jagged like,
    I'd make a great ado.

"So make of me a punkin face—
    A grin from ear to ear;
A nose that I can
    breathe aright,
    And I need have no fear.

"You can punch
    my face with forty holes
    And make me shiny eyes,
But do not gouge my inside out
    To make a punkin pie."

Halloween Customs and Lore

■ In Yorkshire, England, for a time, Halloween was known as "Cake Night," and it was the custom of the mother of every household to bake a special cake for each member of the family.

■ Another popular pastime of Halloween was for a young lady to peel an apple, making sure that she did not break the entire peel. Then she would hold the spiral peeling on the knife blade, swing it three times over her head and throw it over her left shoulder. It was believed that as it dropped to the floor it would form the initial of her future husband's name.

■ The belief that meeting a black cat would bring bad luck arose in the Middle Ages in Europe. The cat was considered a companion of witches and even their familiars. People believed that a witch could assume the form of a black cat. Therefore, all black cats were suspected of being transformed witches. If a black cat crossed your path, it was considered an omen of bad luck.

■ A traditional Irish custom on Samhain eve was the soliciting of contributions in the name of Muck Olla, a shadowy Druidic figure who would be sure to wreak vengeance on the ungenerous. Muck Olla's vengeance gradually became transformed into the tricks of disappointed human revelers.

A Halloween Apple

We'll hang an apple
    and bite it by turns
And thus find an answer
    that everyone learns
Now, this is not magic,
    so don't feel alarm
For I have the answer
    and you have the charm.

Apples hanging in a row.
Flaming candles all aglow.
Witches flying everywhere,
Magic music in the air.
There'll be mischief now I ween
On this mystic Halloween!

—*Vintage postcard*

Witch Facts

■ Perhaps the most popular symbol of Halloween is a witch riding on a broomstick with a black cat perched behind her.

■ The word "witch" comes from "wicca," an Old English word for sorceress or sorcerer.

■ The association of Halloween with witchcraft dates back to both pagan and Christian times. October 31 was the traditional night when evil witches and devils gathered to mock the Church's festival on the eve of All Saints Day by unholy revels of their own. Halloween became the great "witch night" and one of the four principal witches' seasonal Sabbaths was held on this night. These large witches' meetings with the devil were the scenes of excessive feasting, dancing and revelry. It is said that witches would fly on their broomsticks to attend those Sabbaths held far away.

Wicked Witch

Three Little Witches

Marjorie Barrows

One little, two little,
    Three little witches
Fly over haystacks,
    Fly over ditches,
Slide down the moon
    Without any hitches,
Hey-ho! Halloween's here!

Horned owl's hooting it's
    Time to go riding!
Deep in the shadows are
    Black bats hiding,
With gay little goblins
    Sliding, gliding,
Hey-ho! Halloween's here!

Stand on your head with a
    Lopsided wiggle,
Tickle your little black
    Cats till they giggle,
Swish through the clouds
    With a higgledy-piggle!
Hey-ho! Halloween's here!

Dust off the silvery stars
    Till they're gleaming,
Down where the will-o'-wisp's
    Beckoning, beaming,
Dance in the dusk while the
    World lies dreaming,
Hey-ho! Halloween's here!

One little, two little,
    Three little witches
Fly over haystacks,
    Fly over ditches,
Slide down the moon
    Without any hitches,
Hey-ho! Halloween's here!

Bewitching Recipes

Witch's Hands

Items you'll need:
    clear plastic gloves
    candy corn
    plain or caramel popcorn
    ribbon

Optional:
    hangtags
    name cards
    plastic rings

Fill the tips of the gloves with candy corns. Fill the rest of the glove with the popcorn. Tie the gloves with ribbon. Place rings on any finger you wish. Add a hangtag for gifts or name cards for placesettings.

Witch's Hats

Ingredients:

1 3/4 cups flour
1 tsp. baking soda
1/2 tsp. salt
1/2 cup granulated sugar
1/2 cup firmly-packed brown sugar
1/2 cup shortening
1/2 cup peanut butter (creamy or chunky)

1 tsp. vanilla
1 egg
2 tbsp. milk
48 milk chocolate kisses

Preheat your oven to 375°.
Combine all ingredients except chocolate kisses in large mixing bowl. Mix until dough forms.
Shape dough into balls, using a rounded teaspoonful for each.
Roll balls in sugar.
Place on ungreased cookie sheet about 2 inches apart.
Bake 10-12 minutes. Remove from oven.
Immediately top each cookie with a chocolate kiss.

Makes approximately 4 dozen cookies.

Halloween Spooks

Eleanor Dennis

Millions and billions and trillions of cats,
    Cackling old witches in tall, funny hats,
Screech owls screeching from the fence post and tree—
    It's Halloween time as plain as can be.
Dim spooky shadows go slithering by
    As black bats and witches go riding the sky;
Get out your costume and join in the fun.
    Don't let spooks scare you, and don't turn and run;
The scary old spooks are just Jerry and John
    With Mom's old percales ripped up and pinned on.
So get out your costume and funny face too,
    To keep folks from guessing that you are just you.

Clown Jumping Over Pumpkin

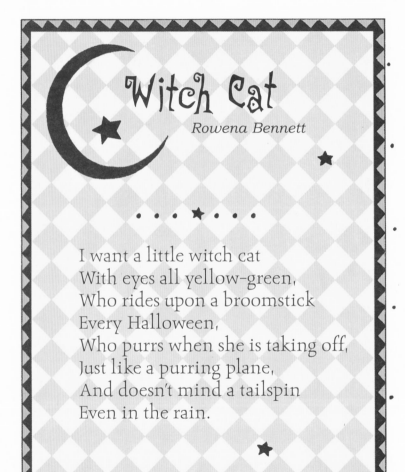

Witch Cat

Rowena Bennett

I want a little witch cat
With eyes all yellow-green,
Who rides upon a broomstick
Every Halloween,
Who purrs when she is taking off,
Just like a purring plane,
And doesn't mind a tailspin
Even in the rain.

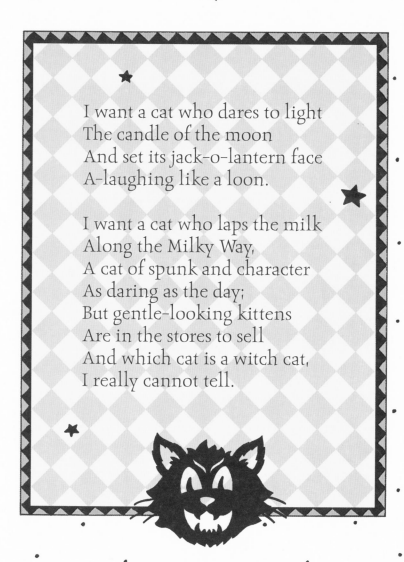

I want a cat who dares to light
The candle of the moon
And set its jack-o-lantern face
A-laughing like a loon.

I want a cat who laps the milk
Along the Milky Way,
A cat of spunk and character
As daring as the day;
But gentle-looking kittens
Are in the stores to sell
And which cat is a witch cat,
I really cannot tell.

Feline Facts

■ The concept of the black cat as a sinister and magical animal is old indeed. Ancient Egyptians worshipped the cat as a deity; in the legends of Greece and Rome, Hecate, goddess of sorcery and patron of witches, chose a woman who had been changed into a cat as priestess.

■ The cat has traditionally been the witch's most frequent companion and helpmate in mischief. With its stealthy grace, demonic glare and fiendish whiskers, it quite naturally became the symbol of Halloween. It was also believed that witches were able to change themselves into cats at will.

■ The widespread superstition that it is bad luck to have a black cat cross one's path comes from the Irish belief that if you meet a cat while on a journey a witch will approach you shortly and bring you bad luck.

Carve Out a Little Fun

The Python
Ogden Nash

The python has, and I fib no fibs, 318 pairs of ribs. In stating this I place reliance On a séance with one who died for science. This figure is sworn to and attested; He counted them while being digested.

Bats
Jamie Curtis

Bats are cute and never scary
  Bats are very sanitary
Bats in dismal caves keep cozy
  Bats remind us of Lugosi
Bats have webby wings that fold up
  Bats from ceilings hang down rolled up
Bats when flying undismayed are
  Bats are careful
Bats use radar
  Bats at nighttime at their best are
Bats by Batman unimpressed are.

The Bad Kittens

Elizabeth Coatsworth

You may call, you may call,
But the little black cats won't hear you;
The little black cats are maddened
By the bright green light of the moon.
They are running and whirling and hiding,
They are wild who were once so confiding,
They are mad when the moon is riding—
You will not catch the kittens soon!

They care not for saucers of milk;
They care not for pillows of silk;
Your softest, crooningest call
Means less than the buzzing of flies.
They are seeing more than you see,
They are hearing more than you hear,
And out of the darkness they peer,
With a goblin light in their eyes!

When the night wind howls in the chimney cowls,
And the bat in the moonlight flies,
And inky clouds, like funeral shrouds,
Sail over the midnight skies—
When the footpads quail at the night-bird's wail,
And black dogs bay at the moon,
Then is the spectres' holiday—
then is the ghost's high noon!

Gilbert and Sullivan's "Ruddigore"

Pumpkin Chariot

Trick or Treat

Going Solo

Patrick Regan

Can you stay on the sidewalk, Mom?
    Can I go on my own?
The big kids all go by themselves.
    I want to go alone.

That old house isn't scary
    I pass it every day
There's no such thing as ghosts or spooks
    I don't care what kids say.

It's dark and kind of creepy, but
    I'm not scared anyhow.
You used to have to hold my hand,
    But I'm much bigger now.

I'll walk right up those creaky steps
And knock or ring the bell
They'll probably be more scared than me
When I jump out and yell . . .

"Trick or Treat!" That's what I'll say,
And they'll give me tons of stuff,
'cause there's no other kids around . . .
Guess they're not brave enough.

What's that?! There's something on the porch!
  Crouched down there on the floor . . .
And are those red eyes that I see
  Peeking from behind that door?

Umm . . . Mom . . . Can you come over here?
  I don't want you to be scared.
Just stand by me and hold my hand.
    . . . I'll go alone next year.

Silly Jokes and Riddles

Why was 6 scared of 7?
Because 7, 8, 9! (7 ate 9!)

Why does the Mummy keep his band-aids in the refrigerator?
He wants to use them for cold cuts!

Where did the witch take her black cat when he lost his tail?
To the retail store.

Where do baby ghosts go during the day?
Dayscare Centers.

Why do witches fly on brooms?
Vacuum cleaner cords aren't long enough.

What subject do witches like best?
Spelling.

When is it bad luck to meet a black cat?
When you're a mouse.

Who won the skeleton beauty contest?
No body.

Why wasn't there any food left at the monster party?
Because everyone was a goblin.

Why do witches wear black capes?
Because they get too hot when they werewolf.

What did the ghost buy for his haunted house?
Home moaners insurance.

Why didn't the skeleton go out on Halloween?
He didn't have any "body" to go with.

Skeletons on Parade

Patrick Regan

Oh, Hear the faint, far-away click-clacking cadence,
    Skeletons on parade!
They march undeterred despite corpus decayance,
    Skeletons on parade!
Chill wind whistles low through their hollow eye sockets,
    Skeletons on parade!
They're ghosts of the dead with unfinished dockets,
    Skeletons on parade!
On ribcage marimbas, the corps plays a dirge,
    Skeletons on parade!
While out of the graveyard, fresh cadres emerge,
    Skeletons on parade!
Hear them cackle and moan as they come into view;
They raise wicked wails in one last ballyhoo.
They're searching for new souls and coming for you!
    Skeletons on parade!

Halloween is coming,
Halloween is coming,
Skeletons will be after you,
Witches, bats, and big black cats,
Ghosts and goblins too—

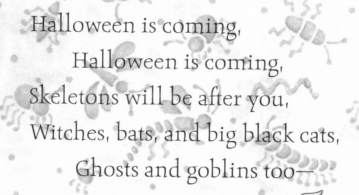

Boo!

Hallowe'en

Fretia Young Miller

While the owls screech
    And the huge bats fly,
The old witch rides
    Her broom thru the sky.

And down in the valley
    In the farmer's corn,
Stands the old scarecrow
    With a goblin's horn.

And while he blows
    There gathers 'round
The eerie ghosts
    Of Cemetery Town.

There also are the
    Green-eyed cats
That paw and yell
    At the huge black bats.

And while I stand
    And gaze at the sky,
The phantoms pass
    Of days gone by.

All the ghosts
    And goblins green
Gather together
    For a fun Hallowe'en.

Trixie and Treat

acknowledgments

Andrews McMeel Publishing has made every effort to contact the copyright holders.

page v, 31, 63, from *Halloween Romantic Art and Customs of Yesteryear* by Diane C. Arkins, published by Pelican Publishing Company.

page 12, "To Pumpkins at Pumpkin Time" by Grace Cornell Tall at http://teachers.net/lessons/posts/202.html:

pages 14–15, Pumpkin Recipes at www.funkins.com/Fun_Page_Recipes.html:

page 19, "Pumpkin Poem" at http://teachers.net/lessons/posts/202.html:

pages 20–21, "Halloween Facts" by Jerry Wilson copyright © 1995–2000 at http://wilstar.com/holidays/hallown2.htm

page 22, "Orange and Black Facts", "Witch Facts", page 32, and "Feline Facts", page 42, are all adapted from *13 Great Ways to Celebrate Halloween* produced by the Halloween Celebration Committee in cooperation with The Toy Industry Association, Inc. copyright © 1983. Reprinted with permission by the publisher.

pages 24–25, "The Legend of the Jack-O'-Lantern" at http://members.aol.com/ezpumpkin/jack.htm

pages 26–27, "The Pumpkin's Wish" by Elsie E. Thornburg, from *Ideals* magazine, September 1956, Vol. 13 No. 5.

illustrations

May Jack-o-lanterns burning bright
 Of soft and golden hue
Pierce through the future's veil and show
 What fate now holds for you.

By goblins of the cornfield stark
 By witches dancing on the green
By pumpkins grinning in the dark
 I wish you luck this Hallowe'en
     —Vintage postcard